ANCIENT EGYPT

A FIRST LOOK AT PEOPLE OF THE NILE

Bruce Strachan

HENRY HOLT AND COMPANY · NEW YORK

For Muila

—————

Henry Holt and Company, LLC
Publishers since 1866
175 Fifth Avenue
New York, New York 10010
www.HenryHoltKids.com

Distributed in Canada by H. B. Fenn and Company Ltd.

Library of Congress Cataloging-in-Publication Data
Strachan, Bruce.
Ancient Egypt: a first look at people of the Nile / by Bruce Strachan.—1st ed.
p.   cm.
ISBN-13: 978-0-8050-7432-1
ISBN-10: 0-8050-7432-5
1. Egypt—Civilization—To 332 B.C.—Juvenile literature. I. Title.
DT61.S887 2006
932—dc2   22005028486

First Edition—2008 / Designed by Meredith Pratt
The artist used mixed media of clay, wood, and oil paint combined with
large-format photography to create the illustrations for this book.
Printed in China on acid-free paper. ∞

1 3 5 7 9 10 8 6 4 2

CONTENTS

WELCOME TO ANCIENT EGYPT

Over the course of three thousand years, the Egyptians built a civilization that continues to fascinate. They erected enormous pyramids that soar toward the stars and constructed elaborate temples in which to worship their gods. Remains of the amazing feats still stand today.

In this first look at the extraordinary world of ancient Egypt, young readers will discover scenes of Egyptian life through rich panoramic dioramas—a unique glimpse into the glory of ancient Egypt and its remarkable people.

THE NILE RIVER

The land of Egypt lies in the dry desert in Africa known as the Sahara. Settlers build homes of earthen walls along the banks of the Nile River. The waters of the Nile make the soil rich for farming, and small villages grow into powerful kingdoms over thousands of years.

PHARAOH

The kingdom of ancient Egypt is ruled by a pharaoh. The people consider him a god. As the supreme priest, the pharaoh is responsible for making sacrifices to the gods to assure the well-being of Egypt.

PYRAMIDS

The Egyptians are famous for building pyramids for pharaohs. The first pyramid-shaped tomb is known as the Step Pyramid. Later, the builders would smooth the sides, but the basic shape remains the same.

Imhotep is the creator of the first stone pyramid. Sand falls through his fingers into the shape of a cone as he dreams of its construction.

Not only an architect, Imhotep is also an adviser to the pharaoh, a healer, and a priest. The people of ancient Egypt worship him as a god.

BUILDING THE PYRAMIDS

Egyptian farmers build the pyramids. They are honored to serve their pharaoh.

Work crews form teams to see who can haul blocks the fastest. The teams struggle under the hot sun to pull three-ton granite blocks up earthen ramps.

THE PYRAMIDS AT GIZA

Behold the pyramids at Giza! They are built as tombs for the pharaohs Khufu, Khafre, and Menkaure. The ancient Egyptians believe each pharaoh is divine. His death is not final; instead, he is reborn after death. Treasures, furniture, clothing, food, and wine are placed inside the royal tomb so that the pharaoh can enjoy earthly pleasures in the afterlife.

Fascinating facts about
the Great Pyramid of Khufu

HEIGHT: Originally 481 feet (more than three times the height of the Statue of Liberty)

WEIGHT: Nearly 7 million tons

NUMBER OF BLOCKS: About 2.5 million

NUMBER OF WORKERS: Between 20,000 and 25,000

TIME NEEDED FOR CONSTRUCTING: About twenty-five years

MUMMIFICATION: THE BLESSING

The body of the pharaoh is preserved for the afterlife by mummification. The inner organs, except for the heart, are removed and placed in special jars. Sweet-smelling incense and oil lamps burn as the priest blesses the pharaoh.

MUMMIFICATION: PREPARATION

The pharaoh's body lies upon a stone table. Priests pack the corpse into a salty mixture, which dries the body of all moisture. This can take up to seventy days.

MUMMIFICATION: PRESERVATION

Next, the priests scrub the pharaoh's body, scent it with perfumes, and rub it with oil. Then they wrap it tightly with fine linen bandages. Good-luck charms are added to preserve admirable qualities, such as beauty and intelligence. A mask portraying the youthful face of the pharaoh is placed over the head of the mummy.

THE BOOK OF THE DEAD

The gods judge the heart of the pharaoh to see if he is worthy of becoming immortal in the afterlife. No pharaoh was ever excused from being judged.

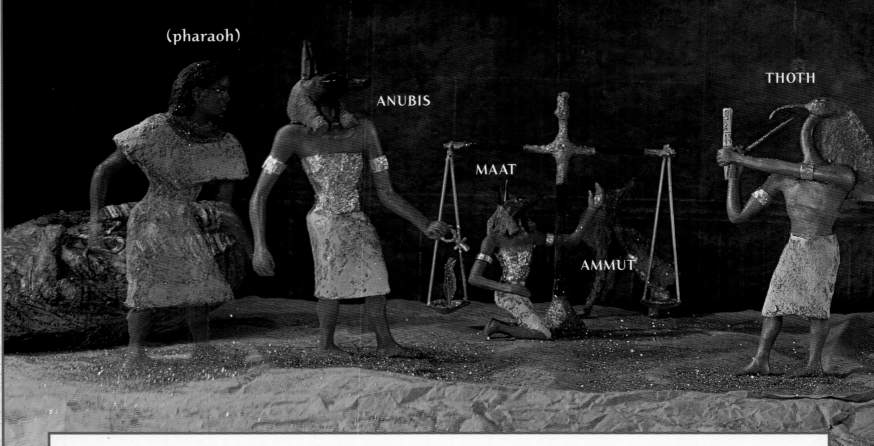

(pharaoh)

ANUBIS

THOTH

MAAT

AMMUT

ANUBIS	The jackal-headed god of the dead	**AMMUT**	The crocodilian goddess
MAAT	The goddess of truth and justice	**THOTH**	The ibis-headed god of writing and knowledge

HORUS   (pharaoh)   OSIRIS   ISIS   NEPTHYS

HORUS   The falcon-headed god of divine kingship

OSIRIS   King of the underworld and god of rebirth

ISIS   Goddess of creation

NEPTHYS   Protector of the dead

THE SPHINX AT GIZA

The Sphinx at Giza is one of the most well-known monuments of ancient Egypt. With the body of a lion and the head of a king, it is 240 feet long and 66 feet tall, carved from limestone, and was originally painted and gilded.

Sitting on the western bank of the Nile, the Great Sphinx faces east to greet the sunrise, the symbol of rebirth and life. Archaeologists believe the monument represents King Khafre, based on the traits of the face and the style of carvings.

QUEEN HATSHEPSUT

The role of pharaoh usually falls to men. Queen Hatshepsut is one of the few women to become a pharaoh. She wears a false beard also worn by male pharaohs. She reigns on her throne as the queen of Punt offers a toy giraffe to her stepson Tutmose III.

RAMSES THE GREAT

With his mighty bow and arrow aimed at an enemy, Ramses the Great charges on his gilded war chariot.

Ramses the Great may have been the ruling pharaoh during the biblical time of Moses. He lived into his nineties and had more than 200 children.

King Tutankhamen's Tomb

After years of digging in the Valley of the Kings, the British Egyptologist Howard Carter is up against a wall. In 1922, along with Lord Carnarvon, Carter uncovers the splendid tomb of King Tutankhamen. Inside, the men find a wealth of objects, including a solid-gold funeral mask, a gilded wood figure of a goddess, lamps, jars, jewelry, furniture, and other objects for the afterlife.

Most royal tombs were plundered by grave robbers, but somehow King Tut's tomb is the only royal chamber that remained relatively untouched for centuries.

In life, Tutankhamen accomplished little, but his magnificent tomb is considered to be one of the greatest archaeological discoveries of all time. In this way, he achieved the immortality and glory desired by pharaohs.

THE FOLLOWING BOOKS AND WEB SITES
PROVIDED BACKGROUND INFORMATION:

Jenkins, Earnestine. A *Glorious Past: Ancient Egypt,
    Ethiopia, and Nubia.* New York: Chelsea House
    Publishers, 1995.
Meltzer, Milton. *In the Days of the Pharaohs: A Look
    at Ancient Egypt.* New York: Franklin Watts, 2001.
Nardo, Don. *Pyramids of Egypt.* New York: Franklin
    Watts, 2002.
Discovery Channel at www.discoverychannel.com.
National Geographic Magazine at
    www.nationalgeographic.com.

THE FOLLOWING MUSEUMS WERE
INVALUABLE TO THIS PROJECT:

British Museum, London; Brooklyn Museum, New York;
Cairo Museum, Cairo; Louvre Museum, Paris; Metropolitan
Museum of Art, New York; Museum of Fine Arts, Boston;
Museum of Nubian Civilization, Aswan; National Museum,
Ethiopia; Peabody Museum, London; Rijksmuseum, Leiden.